FORGIVEN

FORGIVEN

The Power of the Cross

AMBASSADOR INTERNATIONAL
GREENVILLE, SOUTH CAROLINA & BELFAST, NORTHERN IRELAND

www.ambassador-international.com

Forgiven

The Power of the Cross
Conquering Life's Battles

ISBN: 978-1-62020-534-1
eISBN: 978-1-62020-460-3

Cover Design & Typesetting by Hannah Nichols
Ebook Conversion by Anna Riebe Raats

AMBASSADOR INTERNATIONAL
Emerald House
411 University Ridge, Suite B14
Greenville, SC 29601, USA
www.ambassador-international.com

AMBASSADOR BOOKS
The Mount
2 Woodstock Link
Belfast, BT6 8DD, Northern Ireland, UK
www.ambassadormedia.co.uk

The colophon is a trademark of Ambassador

Dedication

This book is dedicated to

Dr. Billy Graham

who has taught me so much about forgiveness

through the power of the Holy Spirit.

Dr. Don Wilton is my beloved pastor and friend.

He continues to be a blessing to me.

Our many times of sharing together

have stimulated my mind and encouraged my spirit.

—Dr. Billy Graham

CONTENTS

THE NEED FOR FORGIVENESS

IT IS ALMOST INCONCEIVABLE TO imagine a five-year-old being forced to watch the brutal torture and murder of his family. But this is exactly what happened to Alex Nsengimana. By 1994, Alex's homeland of Rwanda, in Africa, was plunged into a terrifying and chaotic civil war. Brother was pitted against brother and tribal rage scoured the landscape. Hundreds of thousands of innocent men, women, boys and girls were hacked to death with machetes and their blood flowed like septic poison in open sewers of human decay. The murderers were not strangers; they were neighbors and friends. An estimated one million people lost their lives in the genocide that took place in that country. Alex and his siblings fled for their lives, hiding in ditches and dodging bombs, grenades, and bullets at every turn.

After the war ended, Alex and his brother were sheltered in an orphanage that opened its arms in a loving embrace of those lost and abandoned little ones. After some period of time, Alex was chosen to travel to America to sing in an African children's choir. Despite the song on his lips, the boy was still a casualty of war and suffering insurmountable pain. He was angry, restless, and deeply confused. By God's grace alone, while touring with the choir Alex gave his heart and life to Jesus Christ and found forgiveness for his sins. Soon after returning to Rwanda, he began corresponding with a woman who had housed him in her home in America for two nights when he was traveling with the choir. She offered to sponsor Alex to go to high school in America.

Eighteen years after his family was murdered, Alex went back to his homeland of Rwanda to accomplish a two-fold mission. First, he wanted to "pay it forward" and deliver Samaritan's Purse shoeboxes filled with gifts to the orphanage that had adopted him as a small and deeply damaged boy. Most of all, he wanted to find the man who had brutally murdered his family.

After Alex successfully delivered the shoeboxes, he searched for and found the man, who was serving a life sentence in prison for the crimes he had committed. On that long awaited day, Alex bravely walked up to his family's murderer, face-to-face, and said, "Even though I watched you butcher my family, because of what Jesus has done for me, I forgive you!"[1]

A RIGHT RELATIONSHIP WITH GOD SETS THE STAGE FOR A RIGHT RELATIONSHIP WITH EVERY OTHER PERSON IN YOUR LIFE.

"I forgive you!" These are three of the most powerful words in the universe. They are also three of the most perplexing words we can speak. How does a person come to the point

---

1   Taken from: http://www.samaritanspurse.org/operation-christ-mas-child/alex-story/?utm_source=AlexURL&utm_medium=di-rect&utm_campaign=alex/?utm_source=SPYouTube&utm_medi-um=referral&utm_campaign=m_YTVD-OCCV_medYTvids&utm_content=Love-Your-Neighbor-Alex-Rwanda. Viewed April 7, 2013.

where he is able to truly forgive someone who has brutally murdered one of his loved ones? How is it possible for a person who has murdered an innocent human being to find forgiveness in his own heart? These are complex questions for certain. I think we would be hard pressed to find many people who have not grappled with this issue. Hurt and pain cling to families and individuals like a puppy dog clings to the legs of its owner. It may begin with just an innocent little "yap" but can very quickly become a very painful bite. And, like the puppy dog, hurts can soon grow into a large and very vicious animal that just will not let go. Many families are systematically being destroyed because of this issue. Husbands and wives can find themselves living in the same house and even sleeping in the same bed, but with deep-rooted feelings of resentment that cause even the best to go to sleep with a stone in the heart, only to wake up with a boulder in the heart. Sons and daughters can go for years and years without even talking to their parents because of some hurt or pain that was inflicted upon them when they were simply the young and the restless. The time has come for a fresh new day.

Our Heavenly Father is the author and finisher of our faith. He is the only one who can provide the means by which we can forgive others. He is the only one through whom we can find any means to forgive ourselves. He is the only means by which peace and joy can be restored to our broken and severed relationships. We must look to Him. As you read and study this book, I pray that you will sort out your need to be forgiven, and your need to forgive, in a way that will cause you to rejoice in the power that forgiveness offers.

As we go through this study, I am praying that my words will accomplish a three-fold mission:

> I am praying for a deep desire in your heart to seek God's gift of forgiveness and receive the freedom that it offers.

> I am praying that you will turn loose of the hurt in your heart and seek to forgive those who have sinned against you.

> Moreover, I am praying that you will ask for forgiveness from the people against whom you have sinned.

Receiving forgiveness from God will lead to salvation and a right relationship with Him. In turn, a right relationship with God sets the stage for a right relationship with every single person in your life. These steps build a strong foundation to being completely on the right path in life. All of this is included in the greatest commandment found in Matthew 22:36–39:

> "Teacher, which is the greatest commandment in the Law?" And He said to him, "You shall love the Lord your God with all your heart and with all your soul and with all your mind. This is the great and first commandment. And the second is like it: You shall love your neighbor as yourself."

As we move forward in learning how to receive forgiveness and to offer forgiveness, I will touch on several relevant aspects of forgiveness, but there is so much more. This is a massive subject, with far-reaching implications not only for you but for the many people who are touched by your life. I am praying for you as you seek to understand how forgiveness will influence your life for eternity.

CHAPTER ONE – STUDY QUESTIONS

THE NEED FOR FORGIVENESS

1. Describe a time when you needed to forgive someone. Why do you think it is difficult to forgive?

_____

_____

_____

2. How do you think a right relationship with God will help you have a right relationship with others?

_____

_____

_____

3. Write the name or initials of a person whom you need to forgive.

_____

_____

_____

4. Do you believe that God is willing to forgive you of every sin you have ever committed?

_____

_____

_____

5. Why do you think it was important to Alex to find the man who murdered his family?

_____

_____

_____

6. Read Matthew 22:36–39. How does this verse reveal God's plan for our relationship with Him and with other people?

_____

_____

_____

CHAPTER TWO

THE SALVATION IN FORGIVENESS

EVERYONE NEEDS FORGIVENESS. IT IS a fact that you and I have sinned against God, and we need His forgiveness so we can be in right relationship with Him. Guilt and shame over our wrongdoing may bubble to the surface of our thoughts from time to time, but unfortunately we tend to deny or justify our wrongdoings. One problem with this reaction is that the strength to face our problem and deal with it fades with every denial. Another is that depression and hopelessness can then result from our inner struggle with our guilt and shame.

Possibly, in the deep recesses of your heart, you have buried the need that every person experiences: to have oneness and peace with God. God created humanity with that overriding need, but sin has made it impossible for us to have that peace and fulfillment. Without Jesus' death on the Cross to pay the penalty for our sins, we would have no way to experience it. God affirms the fact of our sin in Romans 3:23, where Paul states, "For all have sinned and fall short of the glory of God." Evidently, and contrary to public opinion, no one is excluded from the scourge of sin. And the consequences are dire indeed!

Many people subconsciously long for the forgiveness of their sins so they can have a deep relationship with God and fulfill the deep needs of their hearts. They simply do not understand that their longing is really a desire for a relationship with God, so they often mistake it for a longing for worldly things. In an effort to find peace and fulfillment, many people search in all the wrong places. To be clear, some of these things are not, in and of themselves, unimportant or insignificant. Some, in fact, are profoundly necessary and noble. But none of these pursuits can offer the peace and satisfaction that can only come by means of a right relationship with God. For example, many people seek important positions in the business world, but they end up at the top of the corporate ladder lonely and still seeking fulfillment. Some people believe that earning a six-figure salary will bring them fulfillment, but they end up spending beyond what they earn, causing them even more anxiety and unhappiness. Some try to win friends and become popular by being the life of the party, but find that even this does not give them peace and contentment. More and more people are turning to illegal drugs, alcohol, and even prescription drugs to alleviate their sorrows, but the drugs and alcohol wear off and they wind up deeper in despair with every episode. Often we seek relationships with the opposite sex, thinking, "If I could just marry him, I wouldn't feel this emptiness in my heart." But soon the honeymoon wears off and that feeling of emptiness returns. None of these things, as good as they can be, can fill the deep needs of the human heart. Only a relationship with God can do that. The one thing that stands in our way is sin. The only hope for removing this barrier is forgiveness of sins by accepting the death, burial, and resurrection of Jesus Christ as payment for your sins.

This need for forgiveness is one of the deepest needs of the human heart. I am often called to the bedside of a dying person by one of their family members, because that person needs to have peace with God before passing into eternity. And the joy of leading a person to Christ on their deathbed is matched only by the joy that wells up within them as they realize God has forgiven them and has "written their names in the Lamb's Book of Life."

Forgiveness, in reality, is God's gift to all people. It is the ultimate mark of His distinctive and amazing love for all people. It reminds me of that great hymn penned by John Newton: "Amazing grace how sweet the sound that saved a wretch like me. I was once lost but now I'm found. I was blind but now I see." Forgiveness lies at the heart of the matter. For, without it, we can never be reconciled to a holy and righteous God. God knows every person intimately. He understands the deep needs of our hearts, and He knows that He is the only one who can truly satisfy our souls. Because of that, forgiveness begins with our relationship with God. When you are willing to face the sin deep in your heart, confess it, and repent of your sin before God. He will forgive you and save you.

God's forgiveness is the starting point. To illustrate God's forgiveness in terms of a baseball game: God is the pitcher, and His forgiveness is first base. We have to receive His pitch of His ball (the Lord Jesus Christ) in order to hit that same ball out into the field of play. None of us will ever get to the first base of forgiveness (which may be with someone very close to us), unless we ourselves have received the only means by which we can be forgiven.

What Christ does for us enables us to do the same for others. Many people refuse to forgive others because they want to make certain that the person who offended them receives due punishment. Wow! I am deeply grateful to God that He does not have the same attitude toward me! God loved us so much that he was willing to receive punishment in our place. In light of this truth, we can see that God's forgiveness is the basis for all other forgiveness.

Here are a few thoughts regarding the benefits of forgiveness:

God cleanses us. Most of us are prone to categorize sin in terms of severity and seriousness. We can certainly understand this propensity. Yes, there are heinous acts committed by people that defy human understanding or logic. It seems that most days include horrible reports of assaults, rapes, violence, and immoral acts of every kind. Society reels and rocks to its core, and people shake their heads in disgust and disdain for the perpetrators of these ghastly acts. Of course it is easy to view these types of things as sin to the nth degree. Our prisons are overflowing with so many people paying the price of their sinfulness. When we consider horrific murders such as beheadings, burning someone alive, or beating someone to death, it is easy to recognize the moral defilement in the heart and mind of anyone who could commit such acts. These "big" sins of society are easy to recognize and condemn, and rightly so. However, what about the "little sins"—as we might mistakenly prefer to call them—such as hate and prejudice? Such sins fill the hearts of many who are considered "good people" and who go to church every Sunday. What about the selfishness and greed of those who live the good "American dream" while their neighbors suffer in great need? Sin is no respecter of persons. The Bible tells us that all have sinned, and when sin is in a human heart, the result is always messy and dirty. Sin makes slaves out of us. It places us in bondage, and only Christ can set us free.

Sin is a serious problem, no matter how major or minor it might be. The Word of God reminds us that "the thief has come to destroy us." Sin is sin. The dilemma remains the same. You can do nothing to cleanse the dirtiness of your sin. You can make a decision to stop drinking, but the addiction remains the same. You can decide to never murder again, but what happens when that overwhelming anger bursts to the surface and you make a snap decision to retaliate physically against someone? You can make a decision to love your neighbor, but if you don't actually love them, the truth will come out. You will never be able to succeed in this area by your own efforts. Repentance is the key requirement. When a sinner is sorry for his sins and asks for forgiveness from God, God is faithful—and able—to forgive that person. God wipes that person's sin away and he becomes as pure and white as snow, in every way.

Forgiveness is one of the greatest miracles ever. And a miracle is something that only God can do. This means that forgiveness is all about God, especially at the beginning.

Forgiveness must start with Him. He forgives us. He indwells us by His Spirit. He enables us to forgive ourselves and others. When Christ died on the cross, He died for every sin ever committed in the past and every sin that will be committed in the future. When we think of all the atrocities and acts of violence that have been committed throughout history, it is overwhelming to think of the magnitude of what Jesus did on the cross. Jesus died on the Cross to save terrorists, murderers, persecutors, and every sinner ever born. God's forgiveness is granted when we confess before Him in full and unbridled repentance. This means we are willing to turn away from our sin and turn towards God. Regardless of the sin in your life, God can and will forgive you. You can become clean and white like the purest of snow.

God frees us. He not only cleans us, but He removes our sin. Sin, in whatever form, fouls us up. But God cleans us and then He eliminates the sin.

What sins have you struggled with? What is your sin tendency? What areas tempt you to sin? What sins seem to cling to you like glue? Are you willing to identify exactly what these things might be in your life? Just as much as we must "count our many blessings and name them one by one," we should also identify those sins in our lives that cause us such grief. It is my firm conviction that Jesus will clean you up and remove the desires for those sins once and for all, if you will surrender your life completely to Him. I have known people who have struggled with addictions all of their lives. One precious lady I know, after many years finally gave up on herself and her own inability to take control of substance abuse. She surrendered her life to Christ. First she confessed her sin to Him. She acknowledged she could not do this on her own. She told the Lord exactly what it was that held her in a vice grip. She repented before God and put her faith and trust in Him. Not only did the Lord forgive her for all her sin, but He forgave her for the specific sins she confessed before Him. A miracle took place: she was delivered and set free. Today this lady is on fire for the Lord. God has changed her, and as a result her entire focus in life has changed. She now helps others to experience the miracles of God in their lives.

Only God can do a miracle like this. However, it requires willingness on the part of the person who has sinned to repent and turn to God.

God restores us. God created you to have a relationship with Him. He also created you for a specific purpose. Psalm 139:16 reminds us that God has every day and every minute and every second of our lives planned out. Sin causes us to get off track and stray from God's plan. But just like your GPS gets you back on track when you have made a wrong turn in your car, so it is that God restores you back to your original track for your life. He gives you a new purpose and a new identity in accordance to his original purpose for your life. He will also use the awful things you have done in life for His glory. The more we sin, the greater His grace—His amazing mercy and supernatural ability to redeem and restore any situation—is seen when He changes our lives. Restoration to the plan and purpose of God takes place because He has set you free. And, just in case of a misguided notion here, this freedom cannot be interpreted to mean "license." Rather, it is the freedom to serve God and to follow His ways and desires for us.

When God forgives, He frees. And when He sets free, He restores. Just like the Psalmist pleaded with God to do after he had committed adultery with Bathsheba, "restore to me the joy of Thy salvation." God removes the prison walls and gives you the freedom to become everything He planned from the beginning. Sin cannot control you any longer. Your old nature cannot control you. You have become "a new creation" (2 Cor. 5:17), and you now have the freedom to be who your Heavenly Father created you to be!

God enables us. When God forgives you, He culminates that amazing act with the enabling power of His Spirit. God moves in to live in you by His Spirit. He takes up residence in you, thereby giving you the ability to function fully, completely, and purposefully. Once again, you become complete in Him. You become whole again. Joy comes back, in full force!

Just as Alex Nsengimana pursued the man who murdered his family, so it is that God pursues you. He longs to forgive you and have a relationship with you. He knows your pain and emptiness without Him. He knows your struggles and your weaknesses. The Holy Spirit calls sinners to repentance. God has a plan for your life and wants you to live it to the fullest. Think about your life today. Do you need to surrender your life to God and receive His forgiveness?

CHAPTER TWO – STUDY QUESTIONS

THE SALVATION IN FORGIVENESS

1. Think of a time when you felt depressed and hopeless because you were struggling with guilt. What did you do to overcome those feelings? Was your plan successful?

_____

_____

_____

2. Describe a time when you tried to satisfy the deep needs of your heart with worldly things.

_____

_____

_____

3. What is the greatest hindrance in your relationship with God right now?

_____

_____

_____

4. Name the things God will do for you when you ask Him to forgive you.

_____

_____

_____

5. Can you remember a time when you surrendered your life to Jesus Christ and asked for forgiveness? Describe what happened.

_____

_____

_____

CHAPTER THREE

THE POWER OF FORGIVENESS

AMERICANS ARE A PEOPLE TRULY blessed. We accommodate and respect other people's differences like no other nation in the world, and—as followers of Jesus Christ—we ought to. A mark of our American distinctiveness is that we respect and honor all people, regardless of what they believe.

I am deeply grateful that I am an American citizen, but I submit to you that this strong desire to accommodate and respect differing beliefs has also led to a blurring of our beliefs about Christianity. By this I mean that many people do not completely understand what it means to be a Christian. They wonder who goes to Heaven and what the significance was of Jesus Christ dying on the Cross. Is there real power in the death of Jesus on the Cross? If so, how does it affect my life?

What we believe about Jesus' death on the Cross is of utmost importance, because what we believe affects how we live our lives. Just suppose that tomorrow pagans took control of our world and announced that they were now in control, much like Muammar Gaddafi was in control in Libya for forty-two years. What if we came under a pagan dictatorship and the pagans dispatched a police force to walk through the doors of your home and into churches all across America with one purpose—to arrest you for being a Christian. Would there be enough evidence to convict you? Have you accepted what Jesus did on the Cross for you? If so, how has it affected your everyday actions?

God says that you can know for sure that you are saved. You do not need to live in a gray world of doubt about your salvation. Maybe you are living out your whole life hovering between two opinions, as many people in America are doing today. Many good people believe their good works will save them. But good works can neither earn our salvation nor gain us entrance into God's presence. Because it is our sin that separates us from a holy and righteous God, it follows that only those who have been forgiven of their sin can be saved for all time and eternity. The only way to receive forgiveness from your sins is through the power of the Cross. Maybe you are giving, serving, and doing all kinds of things to purchase your ticket into Heaven. Quite possibly you believe that if you show good character and integrity, then God will permit you into Heaven? Sadly, many people believe this to be true, and some wish it to be true, so many distinguished religious leaders can be heard explaining away God's plan for our salvation. All across the United States there are people clamoring for someone to justify their "brand" of salvation. One of the many signs of end times is the growing number of people who desperately pursue churches, religious denominations—and even famous clergy members—to justify their sin, ignoring the final authority of the Word of God. Some of the very finest people have died and gone to a Christless eternity because they were not born again of the Spirit of the Living God.

Sadly, there are some churches that operate on the "country club principle." Their members believe that God is going to give them admission into His courts simply because they belong to the church. Americans today are searching for churches that will not threaten their lifestyles. Some seek after churches that offer little challenge to their beliefs concerning salvation. This is very serious business, because it is about life and death. Too many people are being deceived. Too many people are ignoring the truth. Too many people are dying every day and going to a Christless eternity.

THERE ARE FOUR IMPORTANT ISSUES THAT WE NEED TO CONSIDER. These are the source, the substance, the soul, and the search for salvation.

1. THE SOURCE OF SALVATION

People want to know the answer to this most critical question: To whom do we go to find forgiveness? Most people are willing to accept what God says about sin. If, in fact, it is our sin that separates us from God, it follows that the forgiveness of sin and its subsequent total removal and elimination is profoundly important. Who can do this? The answer is, only the Lord Jesus Christ. And while there are many fine clergymen in this world, not one can offer what only Jesus can do. The only way to God is through Jesus, because Jesus is the only Son of God and the only one who paid the price for our sin when He went to the cross. As soon as we rely on any other person, we have a serious problem. All people are the recipients of salvation, but no person is the giver of salvation. Not one single living (or dead) person owns the rights to forgiveness and salvation. So where do we go? We must go straight to God! God has given us His Word as the authority and guidebook for our lives. We go to His Word, because the Bible is absolute truth and inerrant in its teaching.

2. THE SUBSTANCE OF SALVATION

It is simple, really. Salvation is God's act, whereby we pass from spiritual death to spiritual life. In other words, salvation is the guarantee of God that a sinful person has been reconciled to a holy God for all time and eternity. Sin separates us from God. When Adam sinned, death was born, and every person born after Adam has sinned. Humankind is distinct from everything else in creation. Man was created to look like God, to love like God, and to live with God. God created humanity in His image, both male and female. And every person has a mind, body, and a soul. With his mind, man has the ability to think and reason. With his body, man has the ability to work and do good. With his soul, man has the ability to commune with God through the intimacy of His Spirit. Added to this, God gave to man dominion over the fields, over the beasts, and over the earth. He put man in charge of the world. He put Adam in the perfect Garden of Eden. In the middle of the Garden, God put the Tree of Knowledge of Good and Evil. Then He put a prohibition on man. He said, "Don't eat the fruit of the Tree of Knowledge of Good and Evil."

God then put man to work, and gave him the pleasure of marriage. He brought Eve and said, "You two are going to live in a complementary relationship, because I am the God of order." God inextricably intertwined His creation, designed and ordered according to the galactic power of a mighty and a sovereign God. Then God gave to Adam the test of obedience, because God did not create man with a mechanical body operated by a remote control. He gave Adam the choice to obey or not. God did this because true love does not force love in return. God created us to have a relationship with Him, but He wants us to *choose* to love and obey Him.

Then God allowed Satan into Adam's life to test him, but Adam failed the test. He failed in his obedience to a holy and a righteous God. He made the choice to disobey God, thus sin entered his life, and God cast him from the garden—to have no fellowship with Him. However, all the while God was, through salvation in Christ Jesus, reconciling the world to Himself.

Are you a sinner? Did you fail the test? The answer is very simple. Have you ever taken something that did not belong to you? Have you ever told a little white lie or been jealous of your neighbor's material possessions? Of course, we all have sinned in the eyes of God. The Bible says in Romans 3:23 that all have sinned and fallen short of the glory of God. Adam passed the sin nature to all his descendants, down through all generations.

So we all face a great dilemma—there is nothing we can do in our own power to receive forgiveness. We all deserve the punishment of eternal separation from God in a real place called hell. This is why the news of salvation is such good news. Salvation is the divine act whereby God forgives a sinner of his sins and saves him from hell. He then guarantees that person the right for adoption into the family of God forever. It is a divine act of a loving God who is sovereign, but who at the same time gives us a choice to love Him. God, through the shed blood of His own Son, Jesus, and by the convicting power of the Holy Spirit, draws sinful man into relationship with a righteous God.

SALVATION IS GOD'S ACT WHEREBY WE PASS FROM SPIRITUAL DEATH TO SPIRITUAL LIFE.

---

3. THE SOUL OF SALVATION

God is a triune God and that means that God the Father, God the Son, and God the Holy Spirit are all involved in salvation. From beginning to end, every part of God is involved. He is the author of salvation and He is the finisher of our salvation. It originates with Him, it is planned and purposed by Him, and it is only made possible through Him. God cannot be left out or bypassed or considered alongside the opinions of any person, religion, or strong feeling. It is God who loved the world so much that He gave His only Son, the Lord Jesus Christ, in order that all people who believe in Him would not die but would be granted eternal life. It is God, through His Spirit, who convicts us of sin. John 3:16 reads, "For God so loved the world, that he gave his only begotten Son, that whosoever believeth in him should not perish, but have eternal life." The part of forgiveness and salvation that I love so much is that "whosoever" is involved. Who are the "whosoevers?" That is you and me! It is every person on the face of the earth.

Jesus died for all people! Jesus shows us the impartiality of God's divine grace. Yes, all people can be forgiven of all sin. All people can be saved when they meet God on God's terms and not on their own.

The soul of forgiveness and salvation flows from the very heart and soul of our loving and gracious God. It is all about love. Pure love. Real love. What a beautiful thing to contemplate. People crave to be loved. God is love! God has love! God gives love! This is the greatest message that we have—the love of God. Among the countless blessings that Dr. Billy Graham has brought to this world of ours is the constant reminder, "I want you to know that God loves you!" Millions of people throughout the world have received God's full pardon through the forgiveness of their sins after hearing Dr. Graham remind them of this amazing truth. Grace is God's unmerited favor, and God's giving is an act of divine mercy—that God would love us even though we are yet sinners. He sent Jesus, who in full obedience came and died upon a Cross so that we can be reconciled to the Father.

4. THE SEARCH FOR SALVATION

How do we come to know Christ? The Bible is clear. First we must understand some things that are difficult to comprehend. God initiates salvation, in that His Spirit is the one who convicts men of sin and righteousness and judgment. This is something you will know in your heart and soul. Much like the blowing wind, you will know it is blowing, but you may not be fully able to determine where it is coming from. Your heart will be "strangely warmed," as the Bible puts it. God the Father sent His Son, Jesus, who died for your sins. In response to the triune God's work, three very simple acts on your part lead to salvation. These acts are based on Romans 10:9–10:

> because, if you confess with your mouth that Jesus is Lord and believe in your heart that God raised him from the dead, you will be saved. For with the heart one believes and is justified, and with the mouth one confesses and is saved.

We see in Scripture that God outlines the steps to salvation:

Admit before God that you are a sinner. Ask Him to forgive you of the sins you have committed.

Believe with your heart that God sent Jesus to die on the Cross for your sins and raised the Lord Jesus Christ from the dead.

Confess with your mouth that Jesus is Lord.

These three steps will lead you to repentance. When you have asked Jesus to take control of your life, you will have a deep desire to repent—or turn away from—your sins and turn toward God. Repentance means you are coming before the only person qualified to hear your case, and the only person qualified to do something about your case—God.

There are literally thousands of people in America today who have walked down an aisle, raised a hand, gone to a meeting, made a decision, but who do not have a changed life, because they have never allowed Jesus to be Lord of their lives and have never repented of their sins before God. When a person is willing to admit, believe, confess, and repent, there is a difference in their conscience. They come to understand that when they sin, they are flying in the face of the righteousness of a holy God.

So, what must you do to be saved? First, you must admit your sin—acknowledge it. Then you must believe that Jesus died to make the payment for your sins. Then you must confess your sin to Jesus and, in so doing, be profoundly sorry for your sinfulness in His presence. Then you turn from your sin and trust God by faith. You are willing to accept what God says. You take God at His Word. You accept the gift of Jesus in your life and heart. You accept what God has done for you. You trust God to do His work in your life.

You can do this right where you are today. You can get on your knees before the Lord or you can sit right where you are. Talk to God as if He were sitting beside you. Ask Him to save you. Cry out to Him in sorrow over the sin in your life. Ask Him to forgive you for all the sin in your life. Tell Him that you trust Him and you want to live by faith. Thank Him for saving you today.

If you have accepted Christ into your life and God has forgiven you of your sins today, I encourage you to call The Encouraging Word and we will pray with you and send you some information to help you grow in your relationship with the Lord Jesus.

CHAPTER THREE – STUDY QUESTIONS

THE POWER OF FORGIVENESS

1.   Read Revelation 3:15–16. Would you say that your spiritual life is hot, cold, or lukewarm? According to the verses, how does God feel about that?

_____

_____

_____

2.   Where can you find truth about salvation?

_____

_____

_____

3.   In your own words, what is salvation?

_____

_____

_____

4. How is a person saved?

_____

_____

_____

5. Read Romans 10:9–10. According to these verses, have you ever been saved?

_____

_____

_____

6. If you would like to be forgiven and saved from your sins, write your prayer here. Pray according to Romans 10:9–10.

_____

_____

_____

7. Share the good news of your salvation with someone your love. Call or write to The Encouraging Word (our contact information is in the back of this book) and let us know that you have received salvation. We will send you more information to help you grow in your Christian life.

THE ASSURANCE OF FORGIVENESS

PERHAPS THE PREVIOUS CHAPTER OF this book planted some uncertainties in your mind and heart. It is not my desire to put unnecessary doubts in your mind about your salvation, but it is my desire for you to "know that you know that you know" you are saved.

Perhaps you were baptized as a child, but you don't remember knowingly giving your heart and life to Jesus. Maybe you said a prayer asking God to save you, but you never followed through in trusting Jesus on a daily basis. How can you know if you are indeed saved? Is this possible? One reliable way to know is to ask yourself this question: Is my life different now? I didn't say perfect—but different. Ephesians 4:22-24 (NIV) explains this deeper:

> You were taught, with regard to your former way of life, to put off your old self, which is being corrupted by its deceitful desires; to be made new in the attitudes of your minds; and to put on the new self, created to be like God in true righteousness and holiness.

Colossians 3:9-10 (NIV) reiterates the same idea of taking off the old self and putting on the new self:

> Do not lie to one another, since you have taken off your old self with its practices and have put on the new self, which is being renewed in knowledge in the image of its Creator.

If you have walked to the front of the church and joined the church but there has been no change in your life, you might want to reexamine your heart. If you said a prayer asking Jesus to come into your heart but nothing changed, you might want to ask the Lord to show you the truth about your forgiveness and salvation.

Often a person tries to put on the new when they have never taken off the old. Have you ever felt like you had a split personality? Your actions are the same as they were before you were saved, but at the same time, you throw in some good deeds to try to prove your salvation. It is hard to know which person you really are. God's Word explains this further in Ephesians 4:25–32 (NIV). These verses explain how to put off the old way of life:

> Therefore each of you must put off falsehood and speak truthfully to his neighbor, for we are all members of one body. "In your anger, do not sin." Do not let the sun go down while you are still angry, and do not give the devil a foothold. Anyone who has been stealing must steal no longer, but must work, doing something useful with their own hands, that they may have something to share with those in need. Do not let any unwholesome talk come out of your

mouths, but only what is helpful for building others up according to their needs, that it may benefit those who listen. And do not grieve the Holy Spirit of God, with whom you were sealed for the day of redemption. Get rid of all bitterness, rage and anger, brawling and slander, along with every form of malice. Be kind and compassionate to one another, forgiving each other, just as in Christ God forgave you.

When your behavior begins to change and you stop doing the things you did before, then you will have room in your life to put on the new person. Your work ethic will gradually change. Things you did before to cut corners and cheat will bother you once you have the Holy Spirit guiding your life. Your conversation will change. Gossip and unwholesome talk will put a question in your mind that was never there before. When these things begin to happen, then you can choose to put on the new self.

Taking off the old and putting on the new is part of the progressive nature of the Christian experience. What Jesus said to Nicodemus in John 3:3-6 (NIV) may help to explain this more clearly:

> Jesus replied, "Very truly I tell you, no one can see the kingdom of God unless they are born again."

> "How can someone be born when they are old?" Nicodemus asked. "Surely they cannot enter a second time into their mother's womb to be born!"

Jesus answered, "Very truly I tell you, no one can enter the kingdom of God unless they are born of water and the Spirit. Flesh gives birth to flesh, but the Spirit gives birth to spirit.

So the born-again life is not just what you and I have done; it is what we are becoming. Our spiritual growth in the Lord Jesus Christ is progressive in nature. The evidence of being born again, the evidence that I am a "new man" (as the Bible describes believers), is the renewing of my mind and character into the mind and character of Christ. This is the mark of the genuine believer.

How can I know that I am really saved? According to the Apostle Paul, if you are engaged in growing and becoming more like Christ, there will be a new understanding of the death of your old self, with its practices. Once again, God's Word will help in our understanding of this very important stage of our spiritual growth.

In Colossians 3:5-10, Paul encourages the church at Colossae to do the following:

Put to death therefore what is earthly in you: sexual immorality, impurity, passion, evil desire, and covetousness, which is idolatry. On account of these the wrath of God is coming. In these you too once walked, when you were living in them. But now you must put them all away: anger, wrath, malice, slander, and obscene talk from your mouth. Do not lie to one another, seeing

that you have put off the old self with its practices and
have put on the new self, which is being renewed in
knowledge after the image of its creator.

Sadly, there are many people who claim to be Christians,
but it becomes apparent very soon that they have no concept,
understanding, or practice of the death of the old self. Any
person who claims to know Christ but shows no evidence of
this change surely cannot be saved. The old life cannot continue. Business cannot be conducted as usual. If any person
is in Christ "he is a new creation. The old has passed away;
behold, the new has come" (2 Corinthians 5:17). In other words,
spiritually speaking, you will never carry through a resolution
to turn over a new leaf until you rid your life of the old leaf.
You will never make a resolution to turn your life around until
you put it back into its right perspective, which must begin
with putting to death the old self. And get this: it is God, by
His Spirit, who will do this in you. This is not something you
can do on your own. But Christ in you can. He does. This is
how you will know that you are in Him and He is in you.

**THE EVIDENCE OF BEING BORN AGAIN, THE
EVIDENCE THAT I AM A "NEW MAN," IS THE
RENEWING OF MY MIND AND CHARACTER
IN THE MIND AND CHARACTER OF CHRIST.**

When a person has really been saved, you can expect a
new attitude toward other people. Paul says something rather
remarkable in Colossians 3:11: "Here there is not Greek and Jew,
circumcised and uncircumcised, barbarian, Scythian, slave,

free; but Christ is all, and in all." When Paul wrote about the barbarians and the Scythians, he was saying that the Gospel of Jesus Christ transcends even the most unyielding differences among people. According to God's Word, it is biblically impossible to say that you are a born-again believer, and that you are putting on the new man, but to hate someone at the same time. There may be people whom you do not particularly enjoy socializing with because of what they represent. That is a different question. When I discover things about a person that are in diametric opposition to the voice and will of God, I certainly am not supposed to love those things. But at the same time, God's Word says that if I am living progressively, growing in the grace and knowledge of the Lord Jesus Christ, that one of the things I will discover in myself is a new-found love for all people. Some people are jolly hard to love, but the Bible tells us how to love those kind of people. First Corinthians 13 says that love is a direct action, not necessarily a feeling. I love the children's song that says, "Red and yellow, black and white, they are precious in His sight. Jesus loves the little children of the world." Prejudice comes in many ways. Any time you draw a box around yourself and the other person does not fit into your box, there is a great potential for prejudice, whether it be against a different race, culture, age, or nationality. When we truly have been saved, we will have a different attitude toward people who are different.

In John 13:34–35, shortly before He was crucified, Jesus told his disciples that people would know that they are His disciples by their love for one another. If we do not love other Christians, then we may need to reexamine our status as

Christians. The verse reads, "A new commandment I give to you, that you love one another: just as I have loved you, you also are to love one another. By this, all people will know that you are my disciples, if you have love for one another."

When you are truly saved, you will not only have love for other Christians and all people, but you will also have a new understanding of your position in Christ. Colossians 3:12a (NIV) reminds us of that position, "Therefore, as God's chosen people, holy and dearly loved." There are three designations that God gives to those who are in Christ, who are being renewed in knowledge in the image of its Creator. The Bible teaches that after you receive Jesus Christ and as you begin to be obedient to Him, you are going to come to a new level of understanding about who you are and your position in Christ Jesus. God designated you as one of His chosen people—God's elect. Because of Jesus, God's choosing is no longer limited to the nation of Israel; salvation is now available to all people everywhere. Someone said to me, "How do you describe God's election?" It is like journeying down a road and across the road is a big signboard. Right across the highway, it says, "Whosoever to the Lord may come." John 3:16 (NIV) says, "For God so loved the world that he gave his one and only Son, that whoever believes in him shall not perish but have eternal life."

As you journey through this life, the Spirit of God draws you, because you cannot receive salvation outside of the sovereignty of God. God initiates salvation—not you. It is the sovereign work of God. He draws you by the power of His Spirit. His Spirit convicts you, pursues you, draws you, and nudges you into the very heart of God. You repent of your sins. By faith, you receive Jesus into your heart and you begin the journey of eternal life. At that moment, you are saved. As you walk down that road, being renewed in the knowledge of your Creator, you turn around and look back over your shoulder, and on the other side of that billboard are written the words, "You are my elect. You are my chosen one." You have become one of God's elect because He died for you, because that was God's plan for you. As you journey down that highway, you come into a new understanding of your position in God. You are God's chosen one, and you are holy. This means that God has set you apart to use according to His plan. It means that you have a special designation. You have a special determination. You have a special direction. You have a special anointing that God places upon your heart and soul, whereby He purifies you and He makes you to be more like Him. God's Word says you are dearly beloved. God's Word says that when you put your trust in Jesus Christ, you become one of His dearly beloved children.

Can you think of a place where one should be more loved, more accepted, more cherished, than at home? Home is that place where children, no matter what they have done, no matter whose toes they have stepped on, no matter what they have transgressed, know they can walk through that door any time and they've got a neck to hug, a warm bed to climb into, and someone they can share their joys and hurts with. Even when a child has been adopted into a home, they belong. They are loved and accepted and none of that can be reversed. Legally, when a child is adopted, it is a permanent deal. It can only be reversed under strictly defined mitigating circumstances. The

Bible says that when you come to know Jesus Christ, you are adopted into the family of God. When you are adopted into the family of God, you are designated as His chosen one, and this cannot be reversed under any circumstances.

When Jesus Christ comes into your heart and life, He not only saves you from your sin, but He begins to equip you and clothe you by the might and power of His Spirit in your innermost being. He casts your sin as far as the east is from the west and remembers it no more. He provides you with that which is necessary in order to be spiritually and emotionally "clothed" and equipped to lead a life which is well-pleasing in God's sight.

I have very good news for you. God never gives his children hand-me-downs. I came from a home with three boys. To be exact, I came from a preacher's home—I am a preacher's kid. One of the things that I remember quite often was the arrival of a "missionary box." I am not complaining, because those boxes had some wonderful items in them—clothes, food, goodies, and so on. I do have to admit though, that I still have a grudge about those boxes to this day. This is because my oldest brother always got first pick. He got all the good stuff! This used to leave me devastated. Rocky would wear a great pair of pants for two to three years and when he outgrew them, guess who got the hand-me-downs? Little Donald! My mother had this incredible gift of being able to convince me to feel as though the pants I was wearing were brand new pants—despite the holes, grass stains, and fading colors. But God never gives hand-me-downs to His children. The clothes that God gives to us to wear are the very best. Colossians 3:12-14 says:

> Put on then, as God's chosen ones, holy and beloved, compassionate hearts, kindness, humility, meekness, and patience, bearing with one another and, if one has a complaint against another, forgiving each other; as the Lord has forgiven you, so you must also forgive. And above all these put on love, which binds everything together in harmony.

Let me encourage you to get up and dress yourself in the grace of almighty God, in Christ Jesus. Take hold of that which God has made available to you. God desires for you to be clothed, prepared, and equipped properly, so you can face the trials and the tribulations and the ups and the downs of life.

Then Paul gets specific as he begins to name the items we are to put on. I believe that Paul lists them in order to provide just a glimpse of that which God has made available to us.

Compassion is the divine quality called mercy. Compassion is a response to the sick, the elderly, the homeless, the hurting, the abused, and helpless that compels one to respond in a helping way. God's Word says if you are engaged in putting on the new man, you are going to be a person characterized by compassion. Many people think about being compassionate to others but don't follow through, but compassion is a natural result of the work of the Holy Spirit in a Christian's life and heart.

Kindness is a characteristic of the nature of God. Showing kindness involves showing gentleness, benevolence, humanity, consideration, helpfulness, thoughtfulness, and charity. In Acts 4:33, the Bible says that as the believers came together, "great grace" came upon them. I believe that the manifestation of the grace of God is the kindness of a man's heart. The Good Samaritan, whom Jesus described in Luke 10:25–37, was someone who displayed God's kindness when he came to the rescue of the man who had been beaten, robbed, and left for dead. Two other men had ignored the man and walked on by, yet the Good Samaritan stopped, picked him up, and carried him to an inn and paid his expenses. Then he told the innkeeper that he would be coming back and if there were any outstanding expenses, he would gladly pay them.

So when Paul writes in Colossians 3 about being clothed in compassion and kindness, he was not referring to piecemeal kindness. He was talking about the totality and the willingness to pay the expenses after the treatment. Paul talked about going the whole way. He talked about a limitless reservoir.

Gentleness: In my days as a young man, I was dead scared of gentleness. I had the misconception that if I were gentle that would downgrade my masculinity. I believe God does not consider gentleness as being weak-willed and cowardly. Gentleness does not mean you are unwilling to take a stand and to be a man's man and a woman's woman. It does mean that you have that quality whereby you want to suffer in order that other people may not suffer. Gentleness actually speaks to my willingness to take upon my shoulders the burdens that others bear. Gentleness exemplifies appropriate even-temperedness and cooperation when it is for the good of others.

Humility: Jesus humbled Himself, became a man, and took upon Himself the sin of the world. Being humble is recognizing who you are in comparison to God. Humility means accepting your God-given purpose and attributing the glory to Him. It is the opposite of pride and vanity. It is not thinking more highly of yourself than you should. Be careful of false humility. It is easily recognized and is, in essence, the opposite of humility: pride.

Patience is the opposite of revenge. Second Peter 3:15 explains that God is the antithesis of revenge. He is a patient and loving God, and He showed that when Christ Jesus died for us. God has made a way possible for every person on the face of the earth, despite his or her sin, to come into a new relationship with Him. Second Peter 3:9 reads, "The Lord is not slow in keeping his promise, as some understand slowness. Instead he is patient with you, not wanting anyone to perish, but everyone to come to repentance" (NIV). Being patient with others means you will give them another chance, just as the Lord gives us chance after chance to change our ways.

The clothes I wear on the outside are indicative of the person I am on the inside. The Bible says that whatever is in the heart will come out in the actions. Man is limited: he can only look on the outward appearance, but God looks upon the heart. So what is there for man to see that is a manifestation of my heart? It is the clothes I wear, or the outward appearance I portray. I conduct myself in the appropriate manner. Paul says if you are a new person walking in the faith and living for Christ Jesus, there is a new understanding of the death of the old self. There is a new attitude towards all people. There is a new understanding of your position in Christ Jesus; there is a new set of clothes to wear, so to speak.

Then he puts the icing on the cake! He says there is a new reason to forgive others for what they have done to you. Colossians 3:13 (NIV) reads, "Bear with each other and forgive one another if any of you has a grievance against someone. Forgive as the Lord forgave you." In Matthew 6:12, Jesus said the same thing: "Forgive us our debts, as we also have forgiven our debtors" (NIV). If someone you love or care about has ever hurt you, you are possibly thinking, *"How do I forgive this person who has hurt me so badly?"* Paul tells us how to accomplish this. The apostle tells us how to put on the new man. The apostle tells us how to have a new understanding of the death of the old self. He tells us how to develop a new attitude toward all people. He tells us how to have a new understanding of our position in Christ. He tells us how to forgive because God has forgiven us! He tells us how to appropriate and put on the new clothes that God has made available to us.

There are three ways to do this; they are found in Colossians 3:15–17.

First, "let the peace of Christ rule your hearts." The word *rule* means that Jesus Christ is the one whom I call upon to make the judgment, to give direction, to exercise the authority; and when God rules in my heart and life, I become overwhelmed and flooded by His peace and by His grace and I am thereby able to put on the new man. When there is peace in your heart and you have turned everything over to Him, then you have no need to worry about what others have done to you. Forgiving others gives you freedom, and freedom gives you peace. We cannot forgive by our own willpower. Forgiveness is a supernatural act of God through you. When you let go and let God take care of the situation, forgiveness will happen.

This does not mean that you are simply letting the person off the hook to come back and do the same thing over again. What it does mean is that you are allowing God to work in that person's life: administering consequences, healing, forgiveness, or however *He chooses* to take care of the situation. God's discipline is always redemptive, while often ours is vengeful. It is appropriate to set healthy boundaries for your life and family, but God can handle the situation much better than we ever could.

Second, "let the Word of Christ dwell in you richly, teaching and admonishing." Reading and meditating on the Word of God changes a person from the inside out. The Word of God is the offensive weapon in the fight against evil. Jesus used Scripture to overcome temptation in his life. Second Timothy 3:16–17 explains the importance of Scripture. "All Scripture is breathed out by God and profitable for teaching, for reproof, for correction, and for training in righteousness, that the man of God may be complete, equipped for every good work." When you are filling your heart and mind with Scripture and praying Scripture, it is easier to forgive those who have hurt you. This is because God's Word carries God's authority. God's Word is the benchmark for our own sin. When we are able to see our sin when measured against His Word knowing that He forgives anyway, then it is easier to forgive others when they have wronged us.

Third, "Whatever you do, in word or deed, do everything in the name of the Lord Jesus." When you call yourself a Christian, you are representing Christ with your life. When you do not live in a way that is pleasing to Him, it gives the name of Christ a black eye. When you honor Him and obey Him by forgiving others, you are in essence uplifting and honoring His name. The last part of verse 17 says to do everything with thankfulness. Thankfulness is the means by which God's peace, God's Word, and God's name is maintained in our lives. When we trust in God and let his peace rule our hearts, and we dwell in His Word learning how to live, we can put off the old life and put on the new life. When these things happen in your life, it is living proof that you have been forgiven and saved by the blood of Jesus Christ.

CHAPTER FOUR – STUDY QUESTIONS

THE ASSURANCE OF FORGIVENESS

1. Read Ephesians 4:22–32. Name the things in your life that you need to "take off."

_____

_____

_____

2. Name the things you need to "put on."

_____

_____

_____

3. Can you think of any person or group of people whom you hate?

_____

_____

_____

4. Write a prayer to God sharing exactly what is in your heart and mind right now.

_____

_____

_____

5. Read John 13:34–35. Summarize what you read.

_____

_____

_____

6. How are you doing in the following areas?

Compassion –_____

Kindness –_____

Humility –_____

Patience –_____

Gentleness –_____

7. When God looks into your heart, what does He see?

_____

_____

_____

8. After reading this chapter, do you know for sure that you are forgiven and saved?

_____

_____

_____

9. If your answer was "no," reread chapter three again. If you need help, please call The Encouraging Word.

_____

_____

_____

10. Write a prayer to God, letting Him know that you believe that Jesus died for the forgiveness of your sins. Confess your sins and ask Him to forgive you of your sins, inviting the Lord Jesus to come into your heart and life.

_____

_____

_____

CHAPTER FIVE

THE FREEDOM OF FORGIVENESS

IT IS VERY POSSIBLE FOR people who have given their hearts and lives to the Lord Jesus Christ, and who are completely forgiven of their sins, to live the rest of their lives in emotional and spiritual bondage. Many Christians live all their lives needlessly handcuffed and chained to their past. And let's face it: hurts are hard to handle! Pain runs deep, and the devil knows it well enough. All his devices and schemes are brought to bear on the forgiven believer. Open warfare can ensue. The devil makes every effort to chain us to our past while persuading us to fear our future. He brings up our past at every turn in the hope that those memories will cause insecurity to settle in your heart and mind, thus keeping you from pursuing God's will for your life. The devil hopes that, by reminding you of the sins you committed in the past, those memories will cause guilt and shame to blind you to your identity as a child of God. He knows what buttons to push to cause your mind to go back to the past. He also knows how to use people in your life to hurt you. The last thing the devil wants you to do is forgive those people! He knows that refusing to forgive someone plants a seed that grows a bitter root, which in turn produces bitter fruit. Hebrews 12:15 warns against this. "See to it that no one fails to obtain the grace of God; that no root of bitterness springs up and causes trouble, and by it many become defiled." If the devil can prevent you from forgiving those who have hurt you, he knows that not only will *your* bondage continue, it will also be passed down through your children and grandchildren, defiling many generations. The last thing the devil wants is someone with the faith and courage to break the cycle of offense and unforgiveness.

The devil knows that the cycle of sins your family has passed down for many years will cause you to be spiritually weak and unhealthy. How do the sins of one generation affect the next generation? Exodus 20:3,5–6 tells us:

> You shall have no other gods before me. You shall not bow down to them or serve them, for I the Lord your God am a jealous God, visiting the iniquity of the fathers on the children to the third and fourth gen- erations of those who hate me, but showing steadfast love to the thousands of those who love me and keep my commandments.

This is a staggering passage of Scripture. All of us love our children. Most of us understand the extent to which the "sins of the father" can wreak havoc on their children and their children's children. Confession and true repentance before God is the only means by which forgiveness is activated. If I do not obey this commandment, it not only affects me, but it affects my children and grandchildren. God made a dramatic statement when He said, "For I the Lord your God . . . visiting the iniquity of the fathers on the children to the third and fourth generations of those who hate me." It is time to break the chain. Break the cycle. Stop the rot! Eliminate the hurt.

I think of the times I have placed my faith and confidence in someone or something other than God. Then I realize that this is idolatry, and I wonder, "Lord, are you going to punish my children?" Moses settled that question for us. Deuteronomy 24:16 says, "Fathers shall not be put to death because of their children, nor shall children be put to death because of their fathers. Each one shall be put to death for his own sin." God was making it very clear that He has no "family plan" for salvation or for punishment, but He *was* issuing a dire warning. Whether we like it or not, God was warning all of us about the generational consequences of worshipping idols.

Deuteronomy 24:16 makes it very clear that "each is to die for his own sin," but children reared in an idolatrous environment will become infected by that environment. If you worship other gods, you—not God—are the one damaging and thus punishing your children, because they will become practitioners of that environment you create. They will become victims of that environment. In a household where anything or anyone other than God is placed in that one place of worship, the children in that home can grow up and become idol worshipers. Be very careful. Support your favorite sports team, but do not worship it. Enjoy hunting and fishing, but do not worship them. Be appreciative of your possessions, but do not worship them. Earn money and be grateful for it, but do not ever develop an unhealthy love for money. The love of money is the root of all evil (1 Tim 6:10).

CHILDREN REARED IN AN IDOLATROUS ENVIRONMENT WILL BECOME INFECTED BY THAT ENVIRONMENT.

Doing what I am recommending can be hard, because we love our children so much and we think we are doing what is best for them, but we are not. None of these things I have mentioned are inherently bad, but we must be careful not to create an idolatrous environment for our children. God was warning us in Deuteronomy 24:16 not to model idolatry in front of our children, lest they become unproductive adults who believe they are the center of the universe. Children who are reared in idolatrous environments will become victims of that idolatrous environment, and many of them will become idolaters themselves, without even realizing what they are doing. But then, tragically, they will reap the consequences of generational sins passed down in the family, and they will often end up a bitter and dysfunctional adult who has not forgiven their parents.

Maybe you still feel like there is something blocking your joy, peace, and productivity, even though you may have no doubt at all that you are saved. But every time you start to enjoy your Christian life, the devil reminds you of what you did in the past, which in turn incapacitates you with fear, guilt, and regret. Every time you think you have conquered a past sin, it blindsides you by resurfacing in some form or fashion. Every time you begin to serve the Lord, the devil will bring a pawn—some person who is under the devil's influence—who will wreak havoc in your spiritual life. The devil uses people, places, activities, memories, addictions, and anything he can to do his dirty work. Generational sins can be the reason why, even if you have a strong desire to obey God, you cannot seem to stop bowing down to foreign gods, so to speak. Because these idols have been passed down through your family, you cannot get rid of them by simple human effort.

REFUSING TO FORGIVE SOMEONE PLANTS A SEED THAT GROWS A BITTER ROOT, IN TURN PRODUCING BITTER FRUIT.

Quite possibly you have never realized that your past is controlling your future. The enemy will attempt to blind you from the truth while he endeavors to destroy your life and family. Often we are very willing to accept God's forgiveness, but we are unwilling to forgive ourselves. The Bible teaches this truth in Psalm 103:12, "As far as the east is from the west, so far does He remove our transgressions from us." We long for forgiveness and are willing in principle to accept it from God, but in practice we often are incapable of fully letting the past go.

If your past is keeping you bound, I have good news for you. You can break the chains and be free of your past. God has the key that will unlock the handcuffs and remove them for good. You can forgive yourself and those who have hurt you!

I want to share the story of a woman and her daughter, whom I'll call Annie. Annie's mother grew up in a home where family sin had been passed down for many generations. As a result, Annie's mother suffered from depression, anger, and had a deep root of bitterness that prevented her from being the loving mother she knew that God had called her to be. She had accepted Christ as her Savior and she took her daughter to church every Sunday, but anger and bitterness controlled her actions on a daily basis. Annie (of course) saw that her mother's actions were very different at church than at home, and this contradiction caused her great confusion over how a Christian should live. Annie was baptized as a young child, but she did this simply to please her mother; she never really gave her heart and life to the Lord Jesus. Because children learn by example from significant adults in their lives, this little girl learned from her mother to be angry and bitter about her situation. For many years, she actually thought that her life was normal and that this kind of behavior was how all mothers treated their children. Anger and bitterness were such a part of her life growing up that she did not know any other way to live.

As Annie grew up and married, she carried into her marriage the same unchristlike behaviors that her mother had displayed. By God's hand of providence, though, this young woman married a Christian man who had grown up with godly parents. He dearly loved his wife, but after a year of marriage he could not tolerate her anger and hateful actions any longer. One night, in an explosion of anger, Annie dug her fingernails into his face, leaving blood trickling down his cheek. In a scene she had seen played out repeatedly by her mother growing up, she screamed at him, "Go ahead! Hit me! I know you want to!" With a broken heart, he turned to face her and said, "Sweetheart, I have two things to say. First, I will never hit you, and second, I don't see any evidence of Jesus in your life at all." At that moment, the Holy Spirit struck her heart and she knew that her husband was right. She fell on her knees and he led her to accept Jesus into her heart and life that night. She was finally forgiven of her sins.

Did Annie's anger and bitterness disappear immediately? No, it was a process of the Holy Spirit working in her heart and life. God began to orchestrate events so that godly women began to cross her path. These women began to mentor and disciple her. They taught her how to love her husband and her children the way God wanted. This young woman developed a hunger and thirst for God's Word, prayer, and serving the Lord Jesus like she had never known before. After accepting Christ, Annie soon realized that God had given her spiritual gifts and He wanted her to use those gifts to build up the Church, the body of Christ. She began to serve the Lord in every way possible. Soon she and her husband both felt God calling them into the gospel ministry. They both surrendered their lives to ministry and still serve the Lord to this day.

There was one problem with Annie's ministry in those early years. She still had that old root of bitterness and anger, and it would surface at the oddest times. Even though she knew better, her past still controlled her future. The bitter fruit that grew in her life hindered her relationships and ministry. The devil had a foothold in her life and there were times when he would bring up her past sins and abuses. Her bitterness and anger would bubble over, and then for a time she would feel depressed and incapable of serving the Lord the way she wanted to. She would repent in her quiet times of devotion and for a time she would feel better. Then, without warning, her past would resurface and she would again find herself back in the pit of despair. She was ashamed of all this, plus she still had a very rocky relationship with her mother.

Finally, when her desperation exceeded her embarrassment, Annie made an appointment to talk with the pastor of the church where she and her husband served on staff. She shared her whole story and he lovingly led her through the process of allowing the Lord to remove the spiritual and emotional handcuffs and chains that had bound her for many years. First the pastor read Scripture, then anointed her with oil, and then prayed over her. James 5:14-16 (NIV) reads:

> Is anyone among you sick? Let them call the elders of the church to pray over them and anoint them with oil in the name of the Lord. And the prayer offered in faith will make the sick person well; the Lord will raise them up. If they have sinned, they will be forgiven. Therefore confess your sins to each other and pray for each other so that you may be healed. The prayer of a righteous person is powerful and effective.

This young woman was not physically sick; she was emotionally sick. She walked out of her pastor's office with a new heart and mind that day, feeling completely forgiven. She visually put all of the hurts and bitterness into the hands of Jesus. She turned them loose and let them go. She no longer held on to the past.

Her pastor also read 1 Peter 5:8–9a (NIV), that told her how to deal with the attacks of the devil:

> Be alert and of sober mind. Your enemy the devil prowls around like a roaring lion looking for someone to devour. Resist him, standing firm in the faith . . .

Annie started to recognize when the evil one was working in her life and mind, and she began to resist him with the Word of God. She began to recognize idols that were creeping into her life. She read, memorized, and meditated on Scripture to counteract the temptations.

Her pastor read another Scripture, 1 John 4:4, that reminded her that she has victory because the Holy Spirit who lives inside of her is stronger than the enemy: "Little children, you are from God and have overcome them, for he who is in you is greater than he who is in the world."

The wise pastor instructed Annie to go home, sit in front of an empty chair, and "talk" to her mother. This was important because, over the years, Annie's mother had been unwilling to sit down with her and discuss the past. Annie needed to have a conversation with her mother to settle the hurt, so she just pictured her mother sitting in the chair. Then Annie told her mother, out loud, all of the things that had hurt her as a little girl growing up. Then Annie did the unthinkable: she told her mother that she forgave her for each offense in the past and each offense that would occur in the future. After that, whenever her mother offended her again, the offense didn't hurt Annie, because she had already forgiven her mother for it. She had set up healthy boundaries for her relationship with her mother.

This act of forgiveness did not directly benefit her mother, but it benefited Annie tremendously. Her act of forgiveness did not mean that she was letting her mother off the hook by pretending that her mother had not wronged her. It did not mean that Annie became a victim again. It simply meant that she was allowing God to deal with her mother in His way, because Annie could no longer bear the burden. So Annie pictured herself physically taking all the bitterness and anger and all of the myriad of hurts into her hands, raising them up to the heavens, and letting them go into the hands of the Lord Jesus Christ.

The Spirit of God knew what Annie needed and He knows the mind and will of God. He was able to work in her mother's life in a way that only He can do. (God always deals with people redemptively. We, on the other hand, can too often tend to deal with others vengefully.) God continued to work in Annie's mother's heart. Many years later, when she was eighty years old, she approached Annie and asked for forgiveness for the abuse she had imposed on her growing up. Annie, of course, had forgiven her mother many years before and had been healed of the emotional wounds, but it was a blessed day in both of their lives.

Your story may not end as blissfully as Annie and her mother's story did. The offender's actions may never change.

Your forgiveness toward the person is not dependent on their actions, though; it is dependent on your heart and attitude. Forgiveness on your part is not a result of the person asking you for forgiveness; that may never happen. Forgiveness is usually not an instant decision, either; it is a process of working through the results of your hurt.

The results of the offenses against you may have been life-changing or even devastating. I personally know of someone who suffered such an offense: a young man named Brett, who served in the United States Navy. His beautiful wife, eight months pregnant with their daughter, and their sixteen-month-old son were waiting on him to arrive home for dinner, when Brett happened on a robbery attempt and intervened. He was stopped in his tracks by a bullet that ripped through his abdomen, shredding his major organs and severing his femoral artery, leaving him bleeding to death on the pavement.

After twenty days in a coma, multiple surgeries, blood transfusions, and much pain and suffering, God chose to spare his life. But now Brett had to deal with the life-changing results of losing his kidney, a large part of his intestines, and his leg below the knee. This young man has had to work through the process of forgiveness during the past couple of years, but as a result, he and his family are free from the chains of bitterness and anger. The perpetrator never admitted his wrongdoing, and he stood in the courtroom with hatred and vengeance glaring out from his eyes toward Brett. Brett's goal is to visit the offender in prison and extend his forgiveness to him. But, most importantly, he intends to share the grace and mercy of

God with this young man, in hopes that he will receive the forgiveness that will remove his handcuffs, no matter whether he is on the inside of prison walls or the outside. God is using this young Navy man and his family in incredible ways—because of his willingness to choose forgiveness over bitterness.[2]

Because of our human sin nature, having to forgive another person is one of the hardest processes we will ever experience. When we choose to withhold forgiveness, we often think it gives us power over the other person, but in reality, it gives them—and the devil—power over us. When we choose to withhold forgiveness, it not only chains us, it actually chains us to that person. When you choose to hold a person's offense over their head, your thoughts are consumed with that person, chaining you to them like a handcuffed prisoner. Forgiveness frees your mind to think on things that are more important.

God's Word always discloses the answers to life's dilemmas, when we search with all of our hearts. The Lord's Prayer, found in Matthew 6:12–15, tells us that vertical forgiveness requires horizontal forgiveness, "And forgive us our debts, as we also have forgiven our debtors. And lead us not into temptation, but deliver us from the evil one. For if you forgive other people when they sin against you, your heavenly Father will also forgive you. But if you do not forgive others their sins, your Father will not forgive your sins." God forgives us by His grace. Grace is unmerited favor. We do not earn it, nor do we

---

2   Taken from: Brett Parks' *Miracle Man: A Bullet That Ignited a Purpose-Filled Life.* (2015: Ambassador International: Greenville, South Carolina).

deserve God's grace and forgiveness, but He freely gives it to us regardless. So in turn, others may not deserve our forgiveness, but because He showered His grace upon us, He helps us to give grace to others even when they do not deserve it. Vertical forgiveness and horizontal forgiveness frees you and breaks the chains that imprison you.

WE MUST KNOW WHO GOD IS AND WHAT HE IS WILLING TO DO IN OUR LIVES.

In order to forgive and remove the handcuffs, we must affirm a foundational principle. We must know who God is and what He is willing to do in our lives. God is compassionate and gracious. He is slow to anger, but at the same time, He is unfailingly just and wise. He is kind and generous, bestowing all His blessings on us, despite the fact that we are undeserving. God is loving, and He deals with us in a loving way, not a vengeful way. He provides for us completely. He is faithful and His character never changes. His truth will never change. Isaiah 40:6b–8 confirms this: "All flesh is grass, and all its beauty is like the flower of the field. The grass withers, the flower fades, but the word of our God will stand forever."

Finally, God is forgiving. Colossians 2:13–15 (NIV) puts the icing on the cake:

> When you were dead in your sins and in the uncircumcision of your flesh, God made you alive with Christ. He forgave us all our sins, having canceled the charge of our legal indebtedness, which stood against us and

condemned us; he has taken it away, nailing it to the cross. And having disarmed the powers and authorities, he made a public spectacle of them, triumphing over them by the cross.

Wow! He cancelled our sin and nailed it to the Cross. This is the power of the Cross! How can we not let go of the past when the truth is so clear? How can we refuse to forgive others when the nature of God is to forgive all sin? Once you understand this foundational principle about God, then you can begin to work through the process of forgiving yourself, letting go of the past, and forgiving others. You can break the chains and remove the handcuffs!

Do you need to extend grace and forgiveness to someone today? That person may be yourself, or it could be someone who has hurt you in a deep way. Ask the Lord to show you what to do, and then work through the steps of forgiving yourself and forgiving others. It will be a process, but the Lord Jesus will walk by you every step of the way. You will experience true freedom in your heart and a wonderful peace like you have never experienced before.

This is what the freedom of forgiveness is all about. Take hold of all God has done for you. Be forgiven. Give forgiveness. Be free!

CHAPTER FIVE – STUDY QUESTIONS

THE FREEDOM OF FORGIVENESS

1. How does refusing to forgive someone chain you to the past?

_____

_____

_____

2. How do sins of the parents affect their children and grandchildren?

_____

_____

_____

3. What were the steps that Annie's daughter went through to remove her handcuffs from the past?

_____

_____

_____

4. Whom does forgiveness benefit?

_____

_____

_____

5. Read Matthew 6:12–15. What do these verses say about forgiveness?

_____

_____

_____

6. In order to remove the handcuffs, we must affirm God's foundational principle. We must know who God is and what He is willing to do in our lives. Write down everything that you know about God.

_____

_____

_____

7. Name one sin that you need to let go of and forgive yourself. Write a prayer to God about this.

_____

_____

_____

8. How does God's grace to us affect our relationship with others? Do you need to extend grace to someone today? If you can, go to that person and tell them that you forgive them. If it is not possible, find a quiet place and sit in front of an empty chair. Tell them everything you need to tell them. Picture yourself holding on to the offenses. Raise them up and give them to the Lord Jesus Christ. Letting go and giving them to Jesus to handle will give you great freedom.

_____

_____

_____

9. Look back through this chapter and write down the things you need to do in order to remove the handcuffs. It will be a process, but if you ask the Lord, He will walk with you all the way.

_____

_____

_____

10. Talk to God, thanking Him for his forgiveness and grace.

_____

_____

_____

THE HOPE OF FORGIVENESS

NOW THAT YOU ARE WELL on your way in your Christian life, how can you mature and grow as a Christian? God makes available to every single believer five amazing gifts to help you mature. Just as a mother gives her baby all that is necessary to grow, become productive, and stand firm through the rigors of life, God gives us everything we need as well. When you give your life to Jesus Christ, the way of salvation incorporates all that God has done for you. You and I have available to us the most amazing gifts one could possibly ever imagine. As a believer, God drops His anchor into you and pours out His rich grace and mercy through these gifts. As we look at these gifts, begin to think of ways you can incorporate them into your life:

God gives us the gift of His conversation. God speaks to us in many ways. Is that not amazing? God gives to us the remarkable gift of knowing Him intimately through personal conversation. He makes this privilege available to us through prayer. During the time Jesus lived on the earth, the temple in Jerusalem was the center of religious activity. Hebrews chapter nine explains that the Holy of Holies was the place where God's presence dwelled on earth. The Holy of Holies was divided from the other parts of the temple by a thick, tall curtain. Once a year, the high priest could enter through the curtain into the presence of God to make a blood sacrifice for the atonement of sins. Before Jesus died on the cross, only the High Priest had the privilege of entering into the Holy of Holies behind the curtain. But the moment Jesus died on the cross; the curtain was torn in two from the *top to bottom,* thereby signifying that man was no longer separated from God. There was no longer a need to sacrifice the blood of bulls and goats for the atonement, or forgiveness, of sin. The blood of Jesus Christ, shed on the Cross, atoned for all sin eternally. Now we have direct access to the throne of God. We can go into His presence at any time. We do not have to go through the priest, the pope, or a minister; we can speak directly to God in prayer anytime, anywhere. Hebrews 4:14–16 explains this further:

> Since then we have a great High Priest who has passed through the heavens, Jesus, the Son of God, let us hold fast our confession. For we do not have a high priest who is unable to sympathize with our weaknesses, but one who has been tempted as we are, yet without sin. Let us then with confidence draw near to the throne of grace, that we may receive mercy and find grace to help in time of need.

Prayer is an incredible gift whereby we can have an intimate relationship with God. He created us to be in relationship with Him and that is His desire.

God gives us the gift of His Word. The Bible is God's Word to us. The primary means by which God speaks to us is through His Word. The Bible is God's infallible guidebook for

Christians, and you can depend on the truth that comes from it. Not only reading the Bible, but also studying the Bible will give you freedom as a Christian. You will not have to live in bondage to sin, guilt, or shame. John 8:31-32 reads, "So Jesus said to the Jews who had believed in him, "If you abide in my word, you are truly my disciples, and you will know the truth, and the truth will set you free." His word changes hearts and lives. His Word is sharp and teaches, trains, and rebukes our lives.

God gives us the gift of His promises. The Bible is full of promises from Genesis to Revelation—one promise after another. William Carey, an English Baptist missionary born in 1761, said, "The future is as bright as the promises of God."[3] You can trust the promises of God. He will never fail you nor forsake you. He never breaks His promises because it is against His nature. The Word of God is the avenue for learning His promises and trusting Him to do what He says He will do.

God gives us the gift of His Spirit. Every believer has the gift of God's Spirit—the Holy Spirit. The Spirit of God supernaturally enters into your heart and life at the time of your salvation. Because the Spirit of God dwells in you, an unspeakable gift that God gives you is the accompanying power and presence of God in your life, every moment of every day. He will guide you in making godly decisions. He will convict you of sin in your life. He will comfort you in your time of need and trouble. Romans 8:26–27 is one of my favorite verses:

---

3   http://izquotes.com/quote/31501.

Likewise the Spirit helps us in our weakness. For we do not know what to pray for as we ought, but the Spirit himself intercedes for us with groanings too deep for words. And he who searches hearts knows what is the mind of the Spirit, because the Spirit intercedes for the saints according to the will of God.

Wow! This is amazing, if you really think about it. When the Spirit is interceding or praying for you before the throne of God, He knows exactly what to pray. He knows your need and He knows the will of God. When the Spirit puts those two things together and prays before the throne with groanings too deep for words, the outcome has to be God's perfect will for you.

When you give your life to Jesus, repent of your sin, and trust Him as your personal Savior and Lord, His Spirit comes into your heart to reside. He forgives you and writes your name in the Lamb's Book of Life, and then God begins a work in you that lasts a lifetime. Just as a mother takes care of her children, so it is that our Heavenly Father takes care of us His children.

God gives us the gift of His family. When you accept Christ and are forgiven of your sins, you are also adopted into God's family. He becomes your Heavenly Father. Christians everywhere become your brothers and sisters in Christ. God designed the family to nurture and care for one another. He designed the family, especially your church family, to always support and love one another. First Corinthians 12:12–13 reads,

"For just as the body is one and has many members, and all the members of the body, though many, are one body, so it is with Christ. 13 For in one Spirit we were all baptized into one body—Jews or Greeks, slaves[a] or free—and all were made to drink of one Spirit." Verse 27 reads, "Now you are the body of Christ and individually members of it." That chapter goes on to talk about the many different gifts given to the members of the body of Christ. Each person has a role to play in the family of God. We are all different, and God uses each one of us in a specific way to build up the body according to the spiritual gifts He gives us.

The bottom line is this—Christians need one another. We come together as a church to support, encourage, help, and love each other. When Christians gather to worship God, it should be the best time of the week. Often we neglect that gathering and feel like it is not important; but really, it is a God-given gift! When we view other Christians as a part of our family and a part of the body of Christ, it is easier to love each other despite our differences.

As you think about the gifts that the Father has so graciously given you because of your forgiveness, I pray that you will use these gifts and not permit them to waste away as your life goes on. What follows are a number of tangible ways to use the gifts God has so lavishly poured out to you.

Talk to God every day. Every day spend time in prayer with the Lord Jesus. Prayer is not naming a list of things that you need for God to "handle" for you. The purpose of prayer is to have a deep and intimate relationship with God. He longs to know you personally. He longs for you to grow and become who He planned for you to be. God also works in response to our prayers. He has an intricate plan for all of creation, but He also has designed prayer for us to see His power and to know His character. God has the power and the willingness to answer our prayers. Prayer increases our faith and trust in God. Prayer changes our character and actions. Prayer will cause us to be humble when we realize that we are powerless without His Spirit working in our lives.

I see God stirring the hearts of Christians across America to pray. Everywhere I go, I hear of churches and people who are choosing to fast and pray. When God's people turn to Him in prayer, miracles begin to take place. Would you like to see God work His miracles in your life? Would you like to be a part of something bigger than yourself? Make a resolve today that you will have a conversation with your Heavenly Father every day. If you do not know what to say, take your Bible and pray Scriptures to God. The Psalms are filled with wonderful prayers. Psalm 3:3 teaches us this:

> But you, O Lord, are a shield about me, my glory, and the lifter of my head.

Psalm 4:1 reads:

> Answer me when I call, O God of my righteousness! You have given me relief when I was in distress. Be gracious to me and hear my prayer!

What a beautiful prayer! Make a pledge before the Lord Jesus that you will talk with Him every day. I try to set apart some time every day to stop and talk to God. I say something like this, "Lord, I just want to talk to you today. I've got a busy day, and I've got a lot of decisions to make, and I'm facing a struggle. I am hurting, and Lord, I just want to have a conversation with You. I ask You to bless my kids, and do not forget about my grandbabies. Lord, I want You to know I'm praying for America today, and I'm praying for people." Tell Him what is in your heart.

Now that you have accepted Christ into your heart and life, it is important to spend time in God's presence every day in prayer. You can talk to Him as if He were sitting beside you. He hears your prayers and answers according to His riches in glory. Prayer changes your heart and your attitude. Prayer also helps you to see certain situations according to God's purposes. You can approach His throne in your time of need and you will always find mercy and grace. Are you facing battles in life? The Bible tells us in Ephesians 6:12 that our battles are not against flesh and blood, but against the spiritual forces of evil in the heavenly realms. We cannot fight our battles with flesh and blood; we must fight them with spiritual power. A wonderful Christian movie called "War Room" encourages us to fight our battles on our knees in prayer, where we have access to the power of the Holy Spirit. Matthew 6:6 reads, "But when you pray, go into your room and shut the door and pray to your Father who is in secret, and your Father who sees in secret will reward you." Below you will find some strategies to help you begin a regular prayer time with God.

Choose a regular time every day to meet with God in private. If you are a morning person, it is best to pray before you start your day. If you miss your time with God, do not give up. It is like a meal. If you miss a meal, you would not stop eating! Some people are more alert at night and like to pray before they go to bed. The time is your choice, as long as you make it a practice to pray.

Choose a private place. Even though you can pray anytime, anywhere, it is good to choose a place where you are able to focus on your relationship with God. Turn off your cell phone and the television in order to focus completely on His presence. You will find that your mind may wander and you may have many interruptions depending on your season of life. I once heard a young mother say that she had to lock herself in the bathroom in order to pray. While she was praying, she would see little fingers wiggling under the door. Also, distractions may plague your mind with things you need to do, so it may be beneficial to take a pad and paper with you and jot down what you need to do. This will allow your mind to focus back on prayer. When you finish praying, then you can take care of your list of things to do. Having a private place that is comfortable for you will enhance your ability to spend quality time with God in prayer.

Learn to talk to God just as if He were sitting beside you. If you are a new Christian or you have not made a practice of praying, you may feel awkward at first. However, as time goes on you will feel more and more comfortable in praying and it will become natural to you.

You might begin your prayer time with praise for who God is. Thank Him for the things He has done for you. Confess your sins by name. Unconfessed sins will separate you from God's presence. Ask God to bring to your mind ways you have sinned against Him. It is possible to sin and not even know you are sinning. God's Spirit will convict you of sins that you need to confess. You may want to keep a prayer journal to keep you on track in your praying. Here are some ideas for organizing your prayer journal:

- Write your praises to God for who He is.

- Write your thanks to God for the things He has done for you.

- Write your confessions of sin. (You might want to use codes to keep your prayers personal.)

- Share your heart with God. What are you thinking and feeling? He wants you to talk to Him about your life.

- Write the names of your family members whom you pray for daily.

- Write the names of people you need to pray for and their prayer requests. You might pray for certain groups of people on specific days. For example, you might pray for your church staff on Sunday, for your children's schoolteachers on Monday, for missionaries on Wednesday, for government officials on Thursday, and so on. If the prayer requests of other people involve private matters, you might want to write in code in case someone reads your prayer journal. When a person trusts you to pray for confidential matters, it is important to honor that confidentiality.

• Write prayer requests of people who are sick or going through a crisis. You may need to pray for them daily for a time.

When God answers a specific prayer, you can check it off. There is nothing more wonderful than seeing checks in your prayer journal! Those checks remind you that God answers prayers! When you are able to check off a prayer request, always remember to thank God for answering your prayers.

You may have a hard time thinking of things to pray for in the beginning, but soon you will find that you have more things to talk to God about than you have time. Perhaps this is why the Bible tells us to "pray without ceasing." Prayer will change your heart and attitude. Prayer will soon become a vital part of your Christian life.

Read the Bible every day. When a person first accepts Christ as Savior, that person is like a newborn baby. Parents must feed a newborn in order for the baby to grow just as a new Christian must be fed with the truth of God's Word. Reading your Bible every day will feed your mind and heart with the things that will help you grow and mature as a Christian. You possibly may not know where to start when reading the

Bible. It is easy to become overwhelmed when reading some of the Old Testament books even though every book is equally important, and is a part of God's overall story.

I have often heard Dr. Billy Graham tell people to read one psalm and one proverb every day. His reasoning is this: the Psalms teach you how to relate to God, while Proverbs teaches you how to relate to your fellow man. I love that! If you don't know what to do or where to start, I would like to offer you a daily devotional called *The Daily Encouraging Word*. You will find information in the back of this book to order your free copy. When you become a Christian, it is important to feed yourself as a Christian. God takes care of His children. He gave us His Word to feed our souls, minds, and hearts with the important things He wants us to know. The Bible is a guidebook, or map, for life. Without it, we cannot maneuver through the struggles of life.

Trust His promises every day. Trust is renewable every day. There are things that will diminish your trust in God—struggles, hardships, and the battering rams of life. Talking to God will increase your trust level. Reading God's Word every day will increase your trust level. Your level of trust will increase as you fill your mind with His promises every day. The Bible is full of promises. Psalm 119:11 (NIV) reads, "I have hidden your word in my heart that I might not sin against you." The greatest antidote against sin is hiding God's Word in your heart. The more you put God's Word inside your mind and heart, the more the Bible guarantees your ability to withstand those things that the devil attacks you with, trying to break you down.

Join a Bible-believing church and get involved. Gathering as a family with your brothers and sisters in Christ will help you to grow and mature in your faith. Worshiping together, preparing together, serving together, and reaching out to others with the gospel message are all parts of the Christian life. Getting involved in a local church will help you grow and mature as a believer. "Doing life together" with other Christians will help you develop community. When you have developed community, there is where you will find your "2 A.M." friends: those people who care for you so much that you can call them up at two in the morning if you need to. It is in church with other believers that you gather and worship God. His Word tells us to set one day aside to worship Him. When we gather with others to worship Him, we grow stronger as a Christian family.

Live with confidence every day, because you have the Spirit guiding you. You are forgiven! Jesus Christ abides in you, and when the Spirit of God is in you, it does not matter what comes down the pipe; your anchor will hold. The Spirit intercedes for you in prayer and because of that, you are standing on a solid rock. You are unmovable. You are unshakeable. You are undefeatable! You are forgiven, and nothing can stop you from being all that God has planned for you to be!

CHAPTER SIX – STUDY QUESTIONS

THE HOPE OF FORGIVENESS

1. Name the five gifts that God gives you to help you mature as a Christian.

_____

_____

_____

2. How can you develop a strategy for your prayer life?

_____

_____

_____

3. Write a plan for Bible reading and memorization to help you stay on track.

_____

_____

_____

4. Are you an active member of a Bible-believing church? If not, you can call The Encouraging Word and someone will help you find a church close to your home. If you are attending a church, write out a plan to be actively involved. (Attend a Bible study, or small group, or worship service, volunteer in some capacity by joining the welcoming team, or teaching a class.)

_____

_____

_____

5. Write a prayer thanking God for forgiveness. Tell Him what you have learned by reading this book.

_____

_____

_____

CONCLUSION

FOR MANY YEARS NOW I have travelled across the United States sharing the love of Christ with thousands of inmates locked up in our prison system. In the spring, Steve Skinner, my close friend and worship leader, and I minister alongside our seniors, known as Yesterday's Teens. In the summer months we travel with scores of our students, known as Mirror Image. We have been to hundreds of institutions and have seen thousands come to know Christ through the forgiveness of their sins.

In prison, most people understand their need of forgiveness. Outside many do not. The truth is that whether on the inside or the outside, we all need God to forgive us. We have all sinned and fallen short of His glory. For the past two decades, at least, I have always been anxious to get back to Montreat, because I know just how much Dr. Billy Graham relishes talking about this vital ministry of the church he is a member of. As I share the details with him, it seems that he always wants to remind me of all the people he has seen in all the crusades, in all those stadiums, and in all those countries who responded to God's wonderful gift of forgiveness through the Lord Jesus Christ.

"God loves them," Dr. Graham constantly reminds me. "This is why Jesus came and died on a cross for all the people of the world. And He's alive!"

"Don't stop telling them this, Don. Don't stop telling them! This is what our world needs to hear more than anything. Only Jesus can change the hearts of our people—not a president or prime minister, not a preacher, or a pope. Only Jesus. God loves you and wants you to be forgiven!"

And this is what I have just done again. This time I have written some of these truths down. I hope you have read and believed them. But, more importantly, I pray that you have received God's full pardon through the forgiveness of your sins.

NOTES

_____

_____

_____

_____

_____

_____

_____

_____

_____

_____

_____

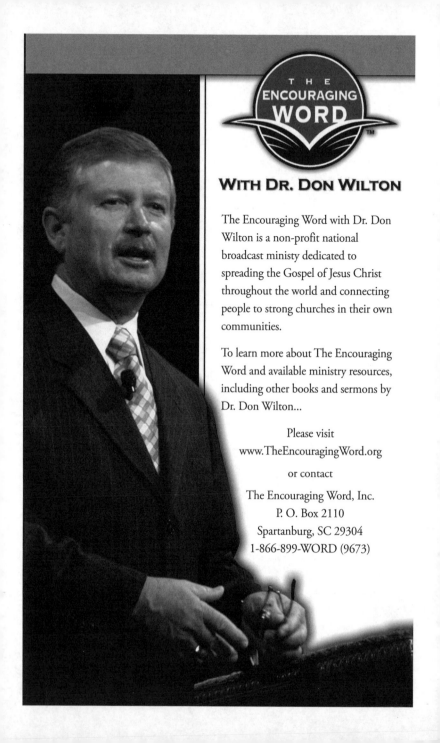

HAS THE ENCOURAGING WORD IMPACTED YOUR LIFE FOR JESUS CHRIST?

SHARE YOUR TESTIMONY WITH US!

"LET US ENCOURAGE ONE ANOTHER..."
HEBREWS 10:25

866-899-WORD (9673)
THE ENCOURAGING WORD
P.O. BOX 2110
SPARTANBURG, SC 29304

WWW.THEENCOURAGINGWORD.ORG

For more information about
Don Wilton
&
Forgiven
The Power of the Cross
please visit:

www.TheEncouragingWord.org

For more information about
AMBASSADOR INTERNATIONAL
please visit:

www.ambassador-international.com
@AmbassadorIntl
www.facebook.com/AmbassadorIntl